THE STAR BEAMS OF LOVE & LIGHT

Laura-Anne Hendry Mooney

Ordering Information:

Prime Seven Media
518 Landmann St.
Tomah City, WI 54660

Printed in the United States of America

Dedications

This book is dedicated to the biggest beam of light, who inspired me to write poetry, my Mum.

Secondly, my Dad, who has supported every word and every day, I have poured into writing this book.

For Mhairi, my best friend forever. Always in my heart with cherry blossoms.

ABOUT THE AUTHOR

When Laura isn't writing, she is walking her dogs. Sweetpea is her toy poodle and her two labradors; brother and sister, Jock and Sally. The dogs are life savers and life givers. A wonderful pack of friends, who all have the most amazing characters and relationships, with Laura and each other. The dogs love to eat treats, run, catch balls, chase foxes and lick Laura's face when they aren't licking each other!

Over the past 10 years, Laura has followed a deep spiritual practice, with meditation, prayer and intuitive guidance being at the centre of her life journey's compass. Picking up a pen to write has always been a part of Laura's life. Although she has shyed away from submitting anything to be put in front of a publisher until the past year or so. Now with a volumetric size of poetry written and short stories, Laura also has a wealth of ideas yet to be written.

The Star Beams of Love and Light is Laura's first brave step into the world of publishing, where Laura hopes to bring a simple spiritual message of love and light, through poetic examples of everyday experiences.

In the space surrounding Earth, across astral vistas, this Universe.

You might just glimpse Star Beams of Love and Light play, dancing across galaxies, our Milky Way.

Sit now still,
with eyes closed softly.
As the Star Beams stream out from the Stars,
in the skies up above.
This is where they beam from
to give you Light and to give you Love.

Now Earth Children,
as you are ready to fall asleep,
you draw magical Love and Light
ever closer, ever near.

These Star Beams are gifted,
with caring thoughts and warm feelings.
Beaming to you from starry,
petal dwellings in our World's sky high ceilings.

Oh, now they are excited, twinkling
and popping out of the sky!

First one, now two and three;
pop, pop, pop!
So full of joy and so full of glee!

The skies are covered in Love and Light,
as the stars they shine, beam and twinkle
sending out Love and Light to you and me.

Let's now see how they do this, as each tells us a
story.

BELIEF, the spark of life, floating upon
a lotus flower.
Radiating light, to your heart, your soul;
sparking your get up and go!
When you are tired and need to sleep,
your soul plays in dreamland,
creating new ideas for you to be, to keep.

To believe with your heart, that your soul lives,
and to love your soul and look after this,
helps belief to twinkle and to exist!

HOPE, so sweet, so small, so neat.
What a gem, for you to keep!

A tiny twinkle, a tiniest of sparks, beamed
down to you in the dark.

For you to treasure, keep safe in your heart.

HOPE will walk with you, light up your eyes,
a purposeful step as you stride.

Use this spark to warm you inside,
when all seems too much,
on the outside.

Remember the 'twinkle',
up it will 'winkle',
warm you it will 'inkle'.

HOPE springs again, and then...

LOVE is in you, please do not doubt.
Loving yourself, a priority for you,
'Little Star Beam Scout'.

LOVE is seeing yourself, as you should be seen.
No space between family, friends and others,
can be felt, or being mean.

Let no hurtful words, fall from your mouth, to yourself.
Loving yourself, closer than your breath.
LOVE magnetises like no other feeling on this Earth!

Love your family. Love your pets.
Your heart beats a frequency beyond your chest.
A special aura, LOVE at its best!

11

For LOVE is here in the now, no next thing or tomorrow.

LOVE is being seen, understood, heard and appreciated for all that you are; even if you don't sing like a bird, or get a grade that misses the bar!

LOVE sends you cherry blossom and bravery thistles, from celestial skies, wraps you in hugs; is there for your smiles, for your cries.

For you are loved child for ALL THAT you are.

Hold onto that knowing, hold on to that feeling,

for this will take you FAR, for LOVE is not fleeting.

LOVE is the highest of feelings.

Always remember LOVE is freeing!

Now GRACE, a cherub face lights up any space, pearl petals, floating down elegantly, surrounding your little pace.

Know as you walk,
GRACE guides your step.

Grace is a feeling, when others can't help, that you can step in calmly, no fuss under your belt, and without even a word no one even asked you for your help.

GRACE glides, not even a whisper,
out comes the splinter,
bandaid applied, tears wiped away,
your little friend helped,
everyone back to play!

Now as Grace passes...

...DIGNITY stands upright, walks strong and tall.

Sends positive vibes to one and all!

At times, when others push and pull you to the ground.

Dignity calls you to get up, walks with you even if you don't FEEL strong and proud.

This is where positive energy can be found.

Look YOUR fear in the eyes,
and with DIGNITY say,
'NO, just STOP, FEAR will not fill ME UP!'

For DIGNITY is with you all lit up,
as your bravery stands strong.
Look fear in the eye, with your own
courage inside, you can do no wrong.

This time fear stands aside,
as you stride forward, you do not run or hide.

When HARMONY appears
sound is cleansed in your space.
Lifting music, allowing flow, timeless pace.

Spending time with you in who you are,
playtime to a place afar.

HARMONY'S notes whistle on the wind,
perfectly attuned to your
special Star Beam airwave spin.

HARMONY'S notes float
gracing the air in rhapsody, whilst

lifting your spirits, your heart, everyday.

Harmony touches with vibration and
frequency, as these special

gifts are given for your unique loving flair;
HARMONY'S sounds are everywhere.

In the wind, CARE blows your needs in front of your wants.
All because your wants may cause you such dismay.

At times emotions may boil up, your senses overcome, wanting things you think will solve your problem.

When really what you truly need
is something completely different, indeed.

CARE will give your need to you,
packaged in a loving way
you won't expect it too!

All of this for your own special care,
wrapped in kindness,
when you least anticipate it,
to be there!

The smile of KINDNESS sends a kiss
through tiny bowed cherry lips.

Puffs of kindness into the sky, colourfully
rainbow high; red, orange, yellow, green,
blue, indigo and violet.

Radiating for all to see, so lovingly.
For kindness is
the kindest action and
feeling a person can be.

KINDNESS shows your colours,
your true beauty shining out!

It doesn't matter
what riches are owned,
or skin tone.

KINDNESS is a currency,
HUMAN electricity!
Radiating colour
between every
HUMAN BEING,
for all of planet Earth to see.

The light of RESPECT waves a fine wand,
showering a wonderful energetic throng.

Guiding you to look after yourself like a
grand piano, a violin, a guitar, or a cello.

For you are the finest of little things;
an instrument made up of beauty,
magic, mystery, yet unimagined
and uncreated beginnings.

RESPECT yourself for you
and all these things,
beautiful child.

RESPECT YOUR FINE INSTRUMENT, YOUR BEING!

For you are full of so much meaning and feeling.

You are an utterly gorgeous
SHINING,
LOVING,
HUMAN BEING...

GIVING is oh so proud, so too is RECEIVE.

With all of your GIVING and RECEIVING,
all of your wondrous BELIEVING!

How amazing you all are to
gift our World by raising
positive vibrations,
through all of your beautiful
thoughts, actions and
feelings!

Raising yourself up in these ways,
helps to keep your energy healthy,
in the most beneficial ways.

Keep up your wonderful self-care,
for these positive vibes work,
they really do! ✷

Calum

The Star Beams of Love and Light are so very, very proud of you and excited to keep shining down and sending gifts to you.

THE END

www.ingramcontent.com/pod-product-compliance
Lightning Source LLC
Chambersburg PA
CBHW040814120626

46547CB00004B/547